Family Talks

poems by

Kevin J. McDaniel

Finishing Line Press
Georgetown, Kentucky

Family Talks

Copyright © 2017 by Kevin J. McDaniel
ISBN 978-1-63534-264-2 First Edition
All rights reserved under International and Pan-American Copyright Conventions.
No part of this book may be reproduced in any manner whatsoever without written permission from the publisher, except in the case of brief quotations embodied in critical articles and reviews.

ACKNOWLEDGMENTS

Thanks to the editors of the following publications in which these poems, some in slightly different form, first appeared:

The Sacred Cow: "Family Talks"—originally published as "Last Supper of a Waning Summer"
Clinch Mountain Review: "The day I thought of the dead" and "Hearing Old Country Superstitions"
Broad River Review: "On Looking at Polaroids"
Appalachian Heritage Writers Symposium: "Rubbernecking"—3rd place, 2017 writing contest

I thank Dr. Parks Lanier, Jr. for his feedback and encouragement, which have helped me grow not only as a writer but also as a person.

Most of all, I thank my wife for her unwavering love and support in this endeavor. I also thank my mother, late father, and siblings for supporting my telling of a few of our family's stories in this collection.

Publisher: Leah Maines
Editor: Christen Kincaid
Cover Art: Amanda McDaniel
Author Photo: Michael Keyes of Photographic Dreams in Radford, VA
Cover Design: Elizabeth Maines McCleavy

Printed in the USA on acid-free paper.
Order online: www.finishinglinepress.com
also available on amazon.com

Author inquiries and mail orders:
Finishing Line Press
P. O. Box 1626
Georgetown, Kentucky 40324
U. S. A.

Table of Contents

The day I thought of the dead ... 1
Preparations for a Child ... 2
Cable Bill ... 3
She named things ... 4
Bumblebees in Hosta ... 5
A Baby Sees Stingrays ... 6
Radioactive Fallout ... 7
A Fat Tick Sucking a Belly ... 8
Family Talks ... 9
Moving ... 10
Coming Out ... 11
Cedar Roots ... 12
Hearing Old Country Superstitions ... 13
Buttercup Warriors ... 14
Fish Friends ... 15
Mermaid at the Aquarium ... 17
Fight in a Station Wagon ... 19
Mrs. Butterworth ... 21
When my father posed beside a mama-san ... 22
Mr. Jones at the Horse Farm ... 23
Hitchhiker Elvis in Memphis ... 24
A good memory rents a house beside bad ... 26
'64 GMC in the Backyard ... 27
Rusty potential ... 28
On Looking at Polaroids ... 30
Rain at a July 4th autograph session ... 31
Throwing rocks at an old house ... 32
Stucco Shack ... 33
Rubbernecking ... 34

The day I thought of the dead

a doctor poked my wife
with an epidural, so she was numb
when she birthed our daughter.
I, dressed in blue scrubs, crouched
behind the bed
and gazed
at the white cover pulled across
her mid-section. Doctors talked about 5 Ks
and weekend retreats, slopped around
cutting instruments and fleshy flaps
during her C-section.

I listened for a baby's cry,
but other voices interjected:
relatives who had worked and retired from jobs,
served in the wars, and played card games
at a picnic table under a maple
whose leaves turned over as signs
of incoming storms
on balmy August evenings—
generations with hands resting
on my shoulders.
I kept feeling my baggy scrub shirt
to find the cross
with Dad's ashes had not fallen
off its clasp
as I strained to hear
my daughter cry.

Preparations for a Child

Clouds checkered
salmon sky like patches
on a homemade quilt
as Tina Turner belted out
What's Love Got to Do With It?

and I chauffeured the car
down roads that cut
through fog before
our unsteady
footprints found
the hospital room

where nurses
huddled to hedge bets—
who could tap
a dehydrated vein
illuminated by
infrared,

and I tried
to deduce the color
of a leaf shimmering outside
the tinted window
when suddenly I heard
your heart harmonize rhythms
on a monitor,

and doctors read
your mother's rap sheet
of medical procedures,
which included a C-section
that pulled you into
this world
that you didn't
ask for.

Cable Bill

I hooted
and hollered when
a cable message
cut in
on cartoons.
I conjured conspiracies
and unpaid bills,
tailgated to
where
you hid hoards
of nickels,
crayons, &
cracker crumbs
in a blue chair.

Entertained
few fleeting minutes,
kicking goals
in imaginary nets,
you rummaged
for my amusement,
but how long
until
you figure
I'm not
the entertainer
you knew
way back then?

She named things

like the time
  I climbed a ladder
    to impale an angel on
      the tree's crown.

She pointed
  to iridescent wings
    and named them,
      Butterflies.

Bumblebees in Hosta

In a turtle-shaped sandbox,
my daughter plays
while two bumblebees
seek sanctuary inside
a hosta's lavender bell blooms
whose stems overhang
the turtle's hind legs.

She bellows and bolts
from flying insects,
so I stay silent,
not provoking. She never
looks up, but chooses
to pour sand grains
through an orange sifter
as I stake out
hosta, host
to a squadron
of pests.

A Baby Sees Stingrays
For Poppas

Scuba divers scrubbed algae
   coating artificial reef pieces
      inside the murky lagoon
         while divers with red tanks
lightly poked pointer sticks
   at nosy green morays.
      When stingrays flattened out
         like ornate gray tapestries

against aquarium acrylic,
   you yanked my shirt collar,
      buried a runny nose
         in my chest.
Your legs pumped
   as if running sprints
      away from fear.
         But in coming years,

you'll welcome
   large eagle-nosed rays
      to glide in front
         of your view
needing
   occasional
      obstructions
         that hide,

and make you forget
   for a time,
      circling sand tiger sharks
         and hovering barracuda
until you can lay hold
   of a diver's pointer stick
      to redirect threats
         that will lie and wait

in your lagoon.

Radioactive Fallout

In early mornings,
I peek through window blinds
to see radioactive fallout
or Vesuvian volcanic ash,
a powdery coat
on windshields and wiper blades,
dryer lint
on the grass.
I stay inside
to fortify air ducts
with black gorilla tape,
building a makeshift tent
out of old flannel
and wine-stained sheets,
dumping a dresser drawer
to hold over my head
inside a closet
with the wife, kid, and dogs,
hoping our little girl will keep faith
because it's pretend until
the dust settles and permeates
everything outside.

A Fat Tick Sucking a Belly

Right there,
under the belly button:
a corpuscular cocoa-colored tick!
Its fat head gulped
bloody baby fat.
I steadied my fingers
to pinch off the head.

Its stubbly legs scurried
and jaws dug in,
too drunk
to give up
the fatty blood bank.
I recalled wild anecdotes
about Lyme disease, Rocky Mountain spotted fever,
and infamous deer ticks.
Legs twitched on the diaper lip.

I phoned the wife:
Hey, babe, can you come home for a little bit?
The baby's got a tick.
...I tried that; couldn't get it.
C'mon, before she gets sick!

She came home,
and with tweezer claws, extracted it,
balled it up in toilet paper,
and lit a match
for the cremation   I witnessed
in the bathroom sink.

Family Talks

We hunted space
nearby a playground where
our little girl shinnied up monkey bars,
so we could talk uninterrupted
under a park pavilion
about Mom's bleeding ulcer,
nieces living
in faraway towns,
and a sister
who issued a death warrant
for a coffee table.
We squeezed dressing
on turkey bacon
in the cornbread salad
and diced yellow tomatoes
for black-bean salsa,
pecked watermelon rinds
and craved toothpicks,
trashed leftovers
when she discovered
the slide.
She jogged in place
at the top. Her tousled hair scattered
as dandelion seeds do in wind gusts.
We took turns catching her
and meditating on
her time
after summer.

Moving
> *For Erin*

When my friends move
to faraway places,

I imagine fountains shooting water
as high as geysers,

coffee houses steaming
the boldest espresso shots,

and house amenities keeping
with modern trends

as I lean on the porch railing
in late evenings

and muse over other reasons for leaving,
my eyes look up

to fog rows coiled in front
of a blue mountain skyline,

which whisper *moving family springs
from selfless necessity.*

Coming out

of the bedroom closet,
our daughter wore a white nylon headband
that pushed up her hair
like the 80's version Cyndi Lauper.

Band-aids,
canvases bearing cartoon characters,
stretched down
her legs
as if
they harbored stories
like old tattoos
before tapering off
at sweaty feet stuffed
in furry slippers.

She asked
for her pink doctor's bag
jammed with
a defunct flip phone, plastic mallets,
yellow spoons with stickers,
and Velcro bracelets.

She was ready
to start the day
(her life),
captured and coddled
by the moment
that will one day hold us captive
when we remember this picture.

Cedar Roots

My family embellished
Christmas trees
with popcorn strings,
cotton bearded Santas,
tangled fat fluorescent bulbs,
and manger scenes—Scotch pines
that my parents bought
at Salvation Army lots.

One year,
I went alone,
all twelve years of me, up on the hillside
where there was nothing
but scrub cedars
and cut one
with a dull hacksaw.

Though a struggle,
I dragged it halfway
before tethering
a dog leash
to the sticky trunk,
which the family dog towed.
Afterward, I dropped the scrub
in a pail wrapped in red Christmas paper
and threw in some bricks.
Prickly branches blinked,
candy canes hung haphazardly,
and fuzzy cotton balls, on the tips,
reminded me of snow.

I had
my own Christmas tree
in my room, spending December evenings
staring up at ceiling cracks
and studying webs
of blinking lights.

Cutting became a tradition,
and I, some years,
return to that.

Hearing Old Country Superstitions

Old superstitions have life after talks
of catchy restaurant names like *Tara Jean's*
or *Old Mill* on a metallic green road sign,

after attempts to ignore radio static,
following labyrinthian segues of plans
for after we pull into a hotel parking lot

with travelers who navigated similar static.
Few riders, however, have a mother, as a passenger,
who can breathe life into country superstitions:

Stories about tearing an old dish rag in half
at midnight at a fork in the road where
Old Scratch then appeared,

or tucking a newborn's caul inside a Bible,
a person looked over the child's left shoulder
to talk to the dead beside a tombstone,

and if the Almighty lulled one spouse to sleep,
the other sought the Holy Ghost for the rest of his days.
In a cramped car, riding to a vacation spot

supposed to make passengers forget about home,
I hear my mother's superstitions elbow out static
and sound like prophecy, not like yesterday.

Buttercup Warriors

My mother taught us kids
about yellow buttercups that grew
on wiry stems in the field
behind our old stucco house
most rainy springs.

She told us
if we picked a buttercup,
and rubbed the petals
under our chins,
a yellow glow would appear,
telling who liked eating butter the most.
We liked bearing the badge
of yellow residue
that looked like
hard-boiled egg yolk
because we had a mark
of special distinction.

I look out
at my backyard
flooded
with the same petals
that shine bright as war paint
at Custer's last stand.
They have brought in
dandelions. Today,
the mower massacres their ranks,
but the buttercups will return
to ask me again and again,
"Butter…butter who likes to eat butter,
buttercup?"

Fish friends

    meet on Thursdays
when a U-haul looking truck pulls up

    at the LFS (local fish store)
where a bearded driver with leg tattoos

    knifes open cardboard boxes.
Fish friends stare down

    at white Styrofoam totes
housing bagged blue water.

    Marble angelfish (anything but angelic)
bite and bicker.

    Reef fish painted
purple, gold, black, and red can't see

    fussy freshwater cousins
(black bags over salt heads)

    while schools of tiger barbs nip fins
to pick a pecking order.

    Store workers stand by like MDs
to count numbers

    of feeder goldfish
that arrive DOA

    because high ammonia
spikes oxygen.

    Watching drab orange survivors
dart nervously,

I see Grandma Arlene's
    thick salt-pepper perm again.

She cradles a round goldfish bowl
    as heavy as a bowling ball

with rainbow-colored gravel,
   aluminum foil sheet on top.

She whispers, These are for you,
   Sugar Foot! You look like Ricky Nelson. I love you.

I lift the bowl
   to sunlight.

Two goldfish appear
   plump white wearing red caps.

They are more beautiful than silk,
   finer than a summer salmon sunset.

Grandma passed down
   aquaholism,

but, wives, a man
   could live life far worse:

chain smoking cigars,
   comparing rum labels

in a crowded aisle
   of an ABC,

juxtaposing chain-saw art
   beside busy roads in Tennessee,

or hogging health foods
   that are too gassy.

Let them drink
   fish water.

Mermaid at the Aquarium

An aquarium worker towed a cart
where a tan brunette sat squeezed

in a pink bikini top holding
white seashells over her bosom.

Children scratched at stenciled scales
that checkered her teal tail fin,

paying homage to fiction
in fish flesh.

You questioned water resistance
of orange and yellow makeup

that sparkled under her eyes
and on her cheeks.

We sat on our butts
in front of tall acrylic panels

housing artificial reef
with yellow, blue, and gray fish

where we watched
the summer dive show

of underwater
acrobatic contortions

ending with
the mermaid's circle kiss

that reminded you
of past mermaid love.

When I didn't remember,
you spouted,

What the hell are you talking about?
I always loved mermaids when were kids!

Such is the reason
I bought you the mermaid knickknack

so that you'd always remember,
and I'd never forget,

the authenticity of
make-believe in color.

Fight in a Station Wagon
For Shane

In late August,
sweat stippled our forearms,
and humidity sucked our breath
to belch in our faces
while Mom and Dad packed road rations
in a white Styrofoam cooler:
bottled water, juice boxes, and ham & cheese.
Plastic grocery bags bulged with changes
of clothes.

Wiping fog from her glasses,
Mom looked up to see if our baby brother, shirtless and in a diaper,
had a bottle. During this intermission,
she griped about going anywhere.
We had no AC (really didn't need it back then),
but using open hands to fan ourselves did little
to cool us on the backseat
in spite of rolling down all the windows.

When Dad pushed up his glasses,
the gesture signaled the wagon would soon coast out
of the driveway. That day,
he violated protocol,
demanding we *shut up and be still*
as he peered into the rear-view mirror.
Yet, his eyes tempted us
to peek at the back window where
we heard a wasp belligerently buzzing
as it head butted the glass.

As if a fireball engulfed the car,
we flung open the doors; our feet dropped dramatically
on the blue graveled driveway. From outside,
we watched the wasp dance erratically
in an upper corner of the window.
Mom, with rattles, tried to lure out our baby brother.
He sat still chugging, not yet knowing fear.

After downing the bottle,
he grabbed it by the nipple, and in a drooping diaper,

scaled the backseat, started swinging wildly as if in a bar fight.
Knowing he'd pay the price for walloping a mad wasp,
we waited for him to cry.
He kept swatting air until he got it
under the bottle's bottom logo crosshairs.
Squished guts painted the story
in the corner of the glass.
The little fella had grit and gumption
to use against whatever was necessary to fight,
even when our fearful family abandoned him
on a backseat
to do the dirty work.

Mrs. Butterworth

When Mom and Dad grocery shopped,
Mrs. Butterworth syrup bottles whistled at shoppers.

I, a toddler, jabbered babble when
she called my name and retold my milestones.

I suspected Dad, in the next aisle, animated her voice,
but she spoke convincingly in commercials.
I continued believing.

Now, I mimic munching sounds
for my daughter who feeds cracker pieces
to Winnie the Pooh.

When my father posed beside a mama-san
>"What sticks to memory, often, are those odd little fragments that have no beginning and no end..."
>
>Tim O'Brien, *The Things They Carried*

he flashed
a peace sign in
Vietnam
where jungle foliage
of green mysteries
lay under a bloated, overcast sky
ready to belch hypnotic notes
that beckoned him
and other boys
to join
the fight.

With a green military cap
pulled down
to his eyes
and fatigues
hanging loosely
off his torso,
he looked more
like a bony teenager
who just stepped out
of the dressing room
at a J.C. Penney,
who with a sly smile
looks to his mother
for approval.

Yeah, Dad,
you looked good
beside the mama-san
dressed in a red v-neck
and black slacks.
She, too, wore a broad grin
under the yellowed Asian conical hat,
looking thankful
that she didn't poison you
like Agent Orange.

Mr. Jones at the Horse Farm

Crystallized in
an old photo,
Mr. Jones, a character
in my dad's childhood stories,
models a plaid Frenchman's cap
and white button-up tucked
in khakis with cuffs
at ankles in penny loafers,
flanked by silky brown horses.
In the background, leafy tree heads lean in
as if to frame the shot.

His boys ran
to the horse farm after school
since things were broken at home,
stroking manes, shoeing hooves,
clenching reins to keep
young colts and themselves
from spooking.

As men,
they held the reins
years after Mr. Jones passed,
and longer, after bulldozers plowed the farm
for park baseball fields.

Hitchhiker Elvis in Memphis
In memory of Lacy (Crazy Horse)

Once
a tractor-trailer driver
with the handle Crazy Horse
picked up Elvis
after greasy shit-on-shingles gravy
at a truck stop
outside Memphis.

The trucker needed help,
keeping   clean   between the lines.
Cautioned
that he didn't do
speed.
Had limits.

Hitchhiker Elvis peddled crazy
mansions,
gates,
Cadillac lines—as long as royal fleets,
and comfortable toilet seats.
The 18-wheeler pulled
in front of Graceland's gates
where he chicken scratched a 10K check
on 2-ply TP sheets.

The trucker headed
for home.
But now
The greasy gravy
had somewhere to go!

Circled back
same truck stop:
parked
     sidestepped
lot lizards
one, he swore,
Reba McIntyre
(another story)
(another poem, really)

before
almost starting
a bathroom brawl.

Had to go
walked straight stiff & squeezed
towards the big rig
    sidestepped
Reba
AGAIN!
before rolling
down
the highway
pulling off
at a wooded byway.

He told it
THAT WAY
with a hand shoveling
Levi Garrett.
Our family— SHOCKED,
bawled and caterwauled (love that word).
How did he forget
a 10K check? And???
just go… shit on
Elvis…
like that???

Better than
hearing stories of
speed
keeping the wheels   clean   between the lines.
This much was true.

A good memory rents a house beside bad

when I feel our daughter's plush black bear.
I relive the day we motored through a national park,

                debated buying stuffed animals in the gift shop
                or a baby bath book with bright colors on the front.

A week later, her first toy hung still
in a bag tattooed with *Thank You* inside our closet

                as we visited Dad at a funeral home
                where his face turned cold after only a day.

'64 GMC in the Backyard

Rust
metastasized
from bed to fenders
to under the hood
and down
to the engine block
where it surrounds a numb battery
on which Dad poured soda
and scrubbed
corrosion
with a toothbrush
on Saturdays.

He is gone.
We work now
to brush off
corrosion,
to reminisce
about him shifting gears
in this puke-green hull
that is still here
parked in
snaky weeds growing through
and above the rims
in our mother's backyard.
Memories are not
for sale.

Rusty potential

> "While porches rot and gutters sag with truthfulness
> The blueprints never tell, my father raises
> Palaces of perfection in the suburbs of his mind."
> Parks Lanier, Jr. "Sunday Paper Blueprints"

spat spurts of battery acid
  during a trip to the county dump
where my brothers and I shot put trash bags
  and muscled a dresser to the tailgate's cliff

to baptize the broken heirloom
  into a dumpster for furniture.
We wanted drawers to flap
  like eaglets falling,

but freedom seldom sprouts wings
  inside a dumpster.
We ignored little pieces
  of scrap metal hurdling hard

like Dad overlooking
  the acid fountain spewing
a corrosive shower
  on the engine block

under the hood
  of his rust-encrusted '64 GMC.
For years, greasy mechanics flashed cash
  to buy our dad's neglect,

talked about *souping it up*
  for classic cruise-ins
while Dad talked his blueprints:
  corking the acid stream,

nipping & tucking Bondo
  in a fender,
sandblasting rust,
  repainting original puke green,

and discarding dry rotted tires
  for more Good Years,
but that's as far as he got.
   The truck rests in Mom's backyard.

She sees potential in pictures:
  a jalopy as a water garden feature
and truck beds converted
  to perennial planters for black-eyed Susans.

Potential fosters tomorrow's blueprints,
  all we ever really have and need.

On Looking at Polaroids

Stashed far back
in the kitchen cabinet,
behind the canned goods,
a red, rusty cookie tin
houses old Polaroids.
From time to time, I sit
at the kitchen table with random piles
that I organize into
what looks like decks of cards
from which I draw off the top and study
backgrounds and clothing styles,
while poking fun at facial expressions
before turning them over to search
the flimsy tea-colored borders
for handwritten dates
that give proper context
to my recollection,
but some have faded.
Then, imagining the stacks
illuminated on an I-phone screen,
I push my fingers to widen the frame
so that I can squeeze into the scene
to ask frozen people
whether lines
in their faces tell stories of the moment,
or bear signs of disintegration
that sets in
after the shot.

Rain at a July 4th autograph session

The pilgrimage began
at a building wearing a red tin roof,
where lines meandered
like cornfield mazes in late October,
but we figured out our place
along with other latecomers
who fisted plastic grocery bags
and shouldered knapsacks
of memorabilia.

My brother
in a sweat-spotted gray t-shirt
toted his green Army bag
crammed with die-cast models and action dolls
as our uncle and his son
compared iconic 8 x10s and a baseball
they wanted signed. I kept looking at my yellowed *TV Guide*
animated by Scotch tape
and the sitcom's actors
from my childhood, for a moment
thinking only re-runs and DVDs preserve
characters with perfect physiques
in fictional towns.

We wanted them to stay that way,
so when cold rain rappelled off umbrellas,
I wrapped keepsakes again in plastic
while we all weathered time in a cloudburst
where the signer also got wet
before going inside to tattoo signatures
that I scrutinize and hope
are permanent.

Throwing rocks at an old house

Cousin J.D. and I scoured a ditch for rocks
with sharp edges that splintered glass into shrapnel

after splitting sun-faded window panes
of an abandoned house on Frederick Street

across from Grandma Mary's whitewashed apartment
where her children and grandchildren gathered on a handful

of summer evenings, visits with dramatic denouements,
aunts and uncles huddled around a yellow Pinto and a white Bug

almost parked in the ditch where we hoarded ammunition.
Grandma, in slippers and a pink house dress, puffed Pall Malls,

listened to her adult children recreate romanced stories
of how they grew up in drafty houses, how cups of water

froze at night on nightstands beside bunked beds,
only to thaw before lunch when the sun got good and hot,

and how *Grandma McCauley would get after ya with a rollin' pin by God!*
J.D. and I pretended to stand on a pitcher's mound, going through progressions,

looking over to a fictional first base, then to the catcher's mitt,
before floating a funky curve or zipping a metamorphic igneous fastball

through second-story windows. From time to time,
our dads spun around, pointed fingers and hollered, *Dottie...Susie,*

they need to stop throwin' these damn rocks!
We did, for a time, but lobbed Guerrilla attacks, shattering

weak glass framed by fading window panes.
Cousin Tracy kept score as if we had bought tickets

for the shooting gallery at a carnival. Thick blond locks back in wings,
he puffed out his chest, morphed into Rick Flair: *How about all that woo?*

Stucco Shack

When I pull
   into the driveway
streaked with amber highlights

   of afternoon sunshine,
the stucco shack
   parades poverty

rooted in a field that grows
   as tall as elephant grass where
a lonely car engine sheds rust flakes

   under an arthritic maple,
and a broken truck rests
   on cement blocks.

An orange *No Trespassing* sign
   glows in a window,
the ugly house on a main road.

   Hard spring rains
spackle scars in the stucco.
   Home

for the weekend,
   I return to campus
on Monday,

   backpacking a story
too rich to tell.

Rubbernecking

> "What love brings me here
> still holds with the drift of years
> like cottonwood fluff
> I catch in my hand, let fly."
>   Bill Brown, "Cottonwood"

My wife slowed the car
to a standstill
in front of the house where we kids spent most of our childhood.
A well's rustic hand pump still lives
beside rain-stained stucco. The shed,
where Dad parked the riding lawn mower
and Jim stored his broken Barracuda,
still looks dilapidated and probably harbors descendants
of the bumblebees that once chased our dad
into a blue plastic kid's pool.
Where are the children of days gone by?
I see us running races on the back field grass
that felt like an old shag carpet between our toes.
I hear our sister neigh like a horse
as she bobs her head across the finish line.
I see our dad take breaks from tinkering
on the rusty '64 GMC to catch me from behind
when I sprinted ahead that summer.
Where are the children of days gone by?
On a sunny Saturday morning, I hear Jim, Dad's best friend,
pulling into the gravel driveway, blasting My Girl,
and Debbie's clippers humming during buzz cuts
on the porch. On the hill where Bear, our black Lab,
hunted rabbits, scrub cedars have grown to scoff at dull hacksaws,
but neither fence posts dividing the farmer's field
from our piece of land, nor the bluebird house
that I nailed to one of the posts, is still there.

Kevin J. McDaniel spent much of his childhood growing up in a stucco house on Middlebrook Road in Augusta County, near Staunton, Virginia. He attended Riverheads High School where he played football, track, and participated in forensics, which cultivated his love of poetry. To that, he remarks, "Preparing and then reading Poe's *Annabel Lee* at a forensics meet left an indelible impression on me, one that has stayed with me throughout the years." Later on, while pursuing his B.S. in English at Radford University and then his M.A. at Virginia Tech, he developed a literary palate for Aldous Huxley, Sylvia Plath, Robert Frost, William Wordsworth, and Philip K. Dick.

Family Talks is his first chapbook of poems, some of which draw from his childhood in the "old stucco house" in the poems "Buttercup Warriors," "Stucco Shack" and "Rubbernecking." Other poems in this collection take root in his experiences of being a father, a son, a brother, nephew, husband, and grandson. To that end, the poems range from the birth of his daughters, "The day I thought of the dead" and "Preparations for a Child," to hearing his mother's account of rural superstitions in "Hearing Old Country Superstitions." The speaker in "Hitchhiker Elvis in Memphis" provides a lighthearted memory of his father, but "A good memory rents a house beside bad" gives readers a brief snapshot of the day he visited his father in a funeral home.

For him, a poem is a time capsule where he paints images, or drops in a specific word that serves as a placeholder of a particular time in his life. Yet, the image or word is accessible so that the reader can see his or her own experience. He believes poems have distinct personalities and, therefore, a life that lives on through readers who share in these stops and travels along with the poet.

www.ingramcontent.com/pod-product-compliance
Lightning Source LLC
LaVergne TN
LVHW041600070426
835507LV00011B/1221